THE QUIET
IN-BETWEEN

30 Days of Sacred Wisdom
and Soul Reflections

Vicki L. Dobbs

Wisdom Evolution
Nurturing Body, Mind, Heart & Soul

Copyright @ 2025 by Vicki L. Dobbs

All rights reserved, including the right to reproduce this work in any form whatsoever, without permission in writing, from the publisher, except for brief passages in connection with a review.

Book Design by Elijah Toten

Wisdom Evolution Books

Ask and It is Written Publishing House
San Diego, CA
www.askanditiswritten.com

If you are unable to order this book from your local book-seller, You may order directly from the author.

www.vickidobbs.com

ISBN: 978-1-7373404-8-5

10 9 8 7 6 5 4 3 2 1

The Quiet In-Between: Sacred Wisdom and Soul Reflections

The Quiet In-Between evokes a still presence and the space you need to regroup, gather inspiration, or perhaps open another gateway. *Sacred Wisdom and Soul Reflections* speak to the inner work of transformation that often happens beneath the surface, in the stillness where wisdom speaks and your heart soars. Listen to the space between the words for those ever-present sacred reminders that you are right where you are supposed to be.

Dedication

To You, the Reader
And all the crazy busy folks out
there that just need a reminder,
TO BREATHE…

*"Within the space where silence
lingers, your soul leans close.*

*Words become lanterns and
reminders become wings.*

*Beneath every sound lives a deeper wisdom
that is written in the space between the
words, in the shadows and in the light.*

*Follow this wisdom, it knows the
way your heart longs to go.*

Contents

Introduction	9
1. Let's Begin, Again	12
2. A Fresh Start Is Not a Failed Ending	14
3. New Ruler, New Possibilities	16
4. Redefining What Matters Most	19
5. The Unearthing of You	21
6. Between Burnout and Breakthrough	24
7. Pages You Are Allowed to Tear Out	26
8. Unexpected Roads, Sacred Pivots	28
9. Where the Noise Can't Follow	30
10. Old Stories	32
11. Cater to Your Curiosity	34
12. Let Yourself Be Surprised	37
13. Time - Friend or Foe	39
14. Be Vulnerable, Ask	41
15. Forgiveness is Freedom	43
16. The Possibility Inside Uncertainty	45
17. Embodied Listening	47
18. What You Hold, Holds You	49
19. Faith in the Unfolding	51
20. Walking with Wonder	53

21. Embracing Life's Detours	55
22. Drifting or Directing	57
23. The Truth You've Outgrown	59
24. Seek Serenity in Stillness	62
25. The Journey is Uniquely Yours	65
26. The Spacious Heart of Humility	67
27. You Are Always Becoming	70
28. Embracing Change	72
29. Wisdom Walks with You	74
30. A Place Between Moments	76
The Mystery Is the Way, Unmapped and Unafraid	78
The Heart of it All	80
A Closing Prayer	82
About the Author	83
Other Books by Vicki L. Dobbs	87
Journal Pages	89

Introduction

There is a place we don't talk about often. It isn't marked on any calendar or to-do list.

You won't find it in the noise of your busy-ness or in the clamor of others expectations.

It is there… in that quiet space just before your next breath or right after a tear falls.

It might show up in the light that dances on your wall or when something inside tells you that you have crossed a threshold or moved through a gateway you didn't even know was waiting for you.

This is the sacred place between moments, *The Quiet In-Between*.

This book was born in that place; not in the rush to fix or force or finish, but in the gentle unfolding of presence. It came to me in the whisper of wisdom that I heard when I dared to slow down and listen.

You don't need to come to this book with a plan, there is no 'right' way to read it.

You can open to any page or read page by page to find yourself there, in the soft ache of your becoming, in the tender resilience of your truth, with the courage it takes to simply be present with yourself.

Each reflection in this book is an offering, a reminder that you are right where you are supposed to be.

You are not lost, and it is never too late. You are right on time and in the right place, right now. You may be wounded, but you are healing.

You are unfolding quietly, beautifully, petal by petal in each moment, into the soul of who you already are.

Walk gently here, where you live and breathe, in this quiet place between moments that is uniquely yours.

1. Let's Begin, Again

Some days ask us for bold beginnings, while others simply ask for the courage to begin again. It's easy to believe that if you didn't get it right the first time, or even the fifth, that you must not be ready for the project or challenge you are facing.

Readiness isn't about finding perfection in your actions. It's a moment of willingness when you step into action with the belief that this is right for you.

Every breath you take offers a doorway back into each moment, back into possibility and presence. When you begin again, you don't erase what you've done before. You carry the lessons you learned with you and choose, once more, to meet life with open hands.

Beginning again is not always starting over. Think of the possibility in starting from… a new experience, from greater growth, from your own limitless possibilities. The messiness of what came before doesn't disqualify you from the endzone, it deepens your drive to get there.

Beginning again is not giving up, it isn't about failing. It is a part of the sacred rhythm of life, of learning. Nature teaches this in the reappearance of tiny green shoots pushing through the frost after a hard winter., or in the moment that the tide changes direction. Whether it's a project, a relationship, a habit, or a dream, give yourself permission to begin again as many times as it takes. This is your journey.

2. A Fresh Start Is Not a Failed Ending

Are you facing yet another do-over? It's time to take a deep breath and remember why you started in the first place. What is the dream, the goal, your deep desire?

Patience is a powerful "friend" reminding you that growth, healing, and progress often take time. Breathe, my friend, there is lot's left to try.

Let that thought germinate in your mind for just a moment: a seed doesn't question the darkness before it breaks through the ground, you can trust that there is so much more to come. Trust the process of your own journey, just like you trust that your dreams and desires require their own time to develop, so do you.

What small step can you take to trust the timing of your journey instead of rushing the process? Perhaps you are ready to release the need to control its outcome. Can you find joy in the place you currently are while your future unfolds in its own divine timing?

Patience is not about standing idly by waiting for something to happen. It's about trusting that the work you are doing will bear fruit at the perfect time. A fresh start is never the result of a failed ending. Don't be afraid to begin again, to move on and carry with you the lessons of what has been as you move into what will be.

Tend to what matters with care and devotion, even as you release your expectations of when or how the outcome will unfold. Now your fresh start becomes about you continuing to show up, heart open, knowing the fruits of your labor will ripen at just the perfect time.

3. New Ruler, New Possibilities

Do you feel your success is often associated with tangible achievements? Could it be that real success comes from your own personal growth, resilience, and fulfillment?

The guideposts that others look for or offer; like wealth, status, or recognition, are merely their perception of their own external validations and may leave your spirit hungry for deeper and more nutritious nourishment.

When you redefine what success looks like for you, you gift yourself a new point of view, one filled with greater possibilities. For example, that promotion you got passed over for might just become the catalyst that boosts you toward a more authentic path.

What experiences, lessons, or milestones have brought you the deepest sense of purpose and joy? These are the sacred moments when you expand your capacity for courage, compassion, and wisdom.

Give yourself permission to celebrate your progress, not just your results. Success is found in the person you are becoming, not just the goals you want to reach.

Pull out a new ruler and measure your "success" by the depth of your character, not the length of your resume.

When you honor the small steps, the still, quiet pivots, and the courage it takes to keep showing up even when the road ahead curves out of sight, you will see that your worth has never been tied to titles or accolades.

It's in the quiet moments of persistence and private victories that no one else sees. That's where your real story is being written.

Resume lines fade away and titles are forgotten, but the truth of who you are becoming will echo through every choice you make, every kindness you offer, and every dream you dare to pursue.

Dream on!

4. Redefining What Matters Most

The path of self-discovery is a continuous one. It is filled with possibilities and opportunities for growth and understanding, for new points of view and the always present sacred pivot. Like an archaeological dig, the journey back to you reveals layers of your true nature that have always been there. They are just waiting to be uncovered.

This beautiful journey is not linear. It spirals ever deeper, as you revisit familiar territory with a new point of view and find new places to explore yourself along the way.

When you embrace the process of redefining what matters most, you reveal more of your own hidden strengths and deep desires.

This isn't a reinvention, it is a re-membering, a homecoming of sorts. It is a returning, a coming back to your authentic self. It is remembering the parts you've forgotten, dismissed, or never fully recognized, as they come into focus in this remembering.

These revelations are glimpses of your true essence. It is the truth of who you are beneath the noise of yours and everyone else's expectations.

Self-discovery and redefining what matters most isn't about becoming someone new. It's about deepening your understanding of who you already are.

Welcome 'you' to the party and don't be afraid to show up as the 'you,' you truly are.

5. The Unearthing of You

Creative expression is a powerful outlet for self-discovery and healing. It bypasses the analytical (ego) mind and allows your deeper wisdom to surface and speak. It is a catalyst that helps your emotions flow out in ways that feel constructive and kind.

The masterpieces that move you most are rarely, technically flawless. What lingers in your memory, what stirs your heart, is not the perfectly rendered strokes or polished lines, but the raw, unfiltered truth embedded within them.

They are authentically expressed and carry the fingerprints of the soul of those who birthed them into the world. There are smudges of vulnerability, echoes of longing, sparks of joy or sorrow that cannot be replicated by perfection.

When you allow yourself to create without expectation, without the weight of judgment, from yourself or others, you open the door to inspiration and joy. You step through a gateway into something sacred.

The inner critic, that ever-watchful sentry, softens at the door. Everything grows quiet and time shifts. What once felt rushed or rigid becomes expansive and fluid.

You begin to remember who you are, not the roles you play or the goals you chase, but the essential you; alive in the act of honest, deep, soulful expression. As each moment expands, you return, closer to your true self.

Engage in sacred creativity not for the result, but for the process. Write, paint, cook, garden, or dream and dance. Whatever floats your boat as they say. Let it nourish your soul, lift your spirit, and open you to your own becoming.

You are not creating to be perfect. You are creating to be REAL.

6. Between Burnout and Breakthrough

There are times when life feels heavy, unclear, or off balance. It isn't because you're doing something wrong. It may just be that you are being called back to yourself.

These "wobbles" are threshold moments, the in-between spaces where renewal is not only possible, it happens. It is an essential action to breaking through from where you are, to where you want to be.

Renewal is not always dramatic. Sometimes it looks like resting. Sometimes it feels like slowing down enough to hear your own heartbeat again, and sometimes it's choosing not to abandon yourself in the name of productivity.

When you feel tired, disoriented, or uninspired, ask: "What needs to be cleared? What needs to be rekindled?" Rejuvenation can be as small as a conversation or a walk. It can be as soft as a nap. It is as simple as a quiet yes to rekindling your own energy.

Guess what? You are allowed to refresh without starting over. You are allowed to change your pace without giving up. Every season, even the tender ones, holds potential for restoration.

What feels foggy now may turn out to be the fertile ground for something long-awaited.

In that space between burnout and breakthrough, give yourself permission to breathe, to listen, to feel your way onto the next path, even when it's a bit foggy and you can't quite see the path ahead. Walk on!

7. Pages You Are Allowed to Tear Out

The stories you carry shape what you believe is possible, but not all stories are meant to last forever. Some were written when you were in survival mode. Some got jotted down when you were steeped in fear. There are others in voices that were never your own. When these stories stop serving your highest be-coming, give yourself permission to let them go.

You don't need to drag old identities with you down new paths. You don't have to keep rereading the chapters that break your heart. You are allowed to grieve who you were and still choose a new path to move forward.

This is not a process of forgetting. This is the freedom that comes with saying, "I've outgrown that version of myself."

It's you choosing curiosity over shame and action over inertia, making a conscious choice to explore these limiting beliefs with openness and wonder. Even a small, intentional choice is an act of tearing out that page from the old story and reclaiming your power in the new one you are dreaming.

Write yourself a new chapter, one with more softness, more space, more truth. Remember, just because that chapter was once true, it doesn't mean it still belongs in the story you are writing now.

Dream it, write it, live it, intentionally present with who you are today.

8. Unexpected Roads, Sacred Pivots

Life's journey doesn't always unfold according to what you plan. In fact, some of the most meaningful events come from the detours you encounter, what I like to call a sacred pivot. It might show up as a closed door here or a delayed opportunity there.

What first felt like a dead end when you hit it, might quietly turn out to be a sacred pivot, your redirection onto a new path.

These sacred pivots ask for your trust. They don't always announce themselves as blessings. Sometimes they feel like disappointments or disruption. Stay with it my friend. They just might reveal something deeper, something you would not have discovered if you had stayed at that dead end and simply pondered which direction to turn.

Instead of asking "Why is this happening to me?" Try asking yourself, "What is this offering me?"

Let each dead end, roadblock, or turn be a sacred teacher. Let each shift be a signal that your journey hasn't stalled out, it isn't over, and it certainly isn't broken.

Look forward to the path ahead unfolding mysteriously, beautifully, according to a sacred wisdom that may only reveal itself in hindsight. #See I told you so.

The road ahead may bend and you may double back, but you are still moving forward. Give yourself permission to keep going.

You are never lost, just passing through a sacred pivot as you journey down unexpected roads. Tally-ho and away you go.

9. Where the Noise Can't Follow

Stillness doesn't have to mean silence. It means turning down the volume on everything that pulls you away from your sacred center.

Stillness is the space between demands and the breath you take between decisions. It is the calm that surfaces when you stop trying to be somewhere other than where you are right now.

In the hush between effort and expectation, there is a place where you can meet yourself without distraction.

Stillness is a gentle turning inward, a sweet homecoming to the wisdom that lies within.

It never leaves you, only waits for your return. When you stop chasing the next moment, you will discover the truth that lives in this one.

Stillness lets you feel what you've been avoiding. and invites you back into your body, back into the present moment. When you stop moving out of habit, you can start moving with intention.

The world may not give you stillness freely, you may have to claim it.

It shows up when you take a break or take a walk. Stillness is enveloped in a deep sigh or the moment you sink your body into warm water. These are small moments, silent sanctuaries you create. They are the thresholds you cross or the gateways you move through that take you back to yourself.

Let yourself be quiet enough to hear your own knowing. Let yourself return time and again to that place where the noise can't follow.

10. Old Stories

Inherited stories can become burdensome beliefs when you choose to carry them forward as your own. Some may have been given to you; some you chose to pick up and believe. There are some you have carried to protect you, to help you survive when there was more asked of you than seemed possible for you to do or be.

There comes a time when these old stories no longer fit with the person you are becoming. A belief that once held safety may now feel like a weight draped heavy over your shoulders.

Letting these old stories go is not easy, but it is an act of courage. It is having a deep reverence and trust in your own sacred unfolding. Allow yourself to grieve the characters and history you choose to delete, the stuff you "wrote" into your story back when it felt sacred. Honor your younger self who needed those stories and the chapters you wrote about them.

Now, with tenderness, patience, and joy, release these old stories and let them drift away like autumn leaves in the wind.

You are not erasing your past; you are making space for each new story that is waiting for you to write.

Imagine your heart as the open sky and those old stories are birds ready to fly. Trust that they have served their purpose and let them go.

You are not bound by what you once believed. What you choose to carry forward is yours to shape with courage, love, and determination.

You are free to write again, to begin again, to rise in the quiet in-between, into a beautiful new story that meets your soul where you are now.

11. Cater to Your Curiosity

When is the last time your curiosity captured your attention?

There's something quite fun about looking at curiosity as a sacred practice. It can elevate those everyday moments of wonder you encounter, into something much more profound.

The idea that your questions could be doorways to a deeper understanding of that wonder, feels both inspiring and exciting.

In that space between question and answer, there lies a world of possibilities. Your curiosity is far from just an intellectual pursuit. It is your soul's way of reaching out toward your authentic truth, beauty, and a deeper understanding of your path and purpose.

Curiosity is a whisper of the Divine inviting you to look beyond the veil of the ordinary and allow for the infinite possibility of the extraordinary. It softens resistance and invites you to explore, to discover, and to remain open to all that is and might be.

When you honor your curiosity, you align yourself with the creative spirit that moves through all things. You become a co-creator in the unfolding mystery of your existence, an open vessel ready to receive wisdom, even from the most unexpected sources.

Your sacred wondering asks nothing of you but to stay open and curious with a willingness to see with fresh eyes and an open heart.

When you cater to your curiosity, every moment becomes a doorway to new revelations. The ancient mystics knew this truth: that genuine inquiry, born of curiosity, dissolves the barriers between self and world, between seer and the sought.

Let your curiosity guide you toward what brings you joy. Follow it into what feels off and explore where the balance needs to be restored. Chase it toward what lights up your body when you speak it out loud.

You don't need all the answers. You only need to stay open and willing to ask the next brave question.

12. Let Yourself Be Surprised

Give life a chance to meet you in the mystery, in places you didn't even know you needed to go. Let wonder find you in the small cracks between routines as you let go of needing every step to be mapped out.

Some of the best moments happen not because you planned them, but because you didn't resist them. Let yourself be surprised by kindness, by grace, and even by your own strength.

There is profound wisdom in releasing your grip on certainty. When you let go of your insistence on knowing what comes next, you create a sacred space for miracles to unfold in the unknown and unplanned.

The Universe conspires in ways your linear mind cannot fathom, orchestrating encounters and revelations that arrive precisely when your soul is ready to receive them.

In the gentle surrender of control, you will discover that you are held by something far greater than your own understanding. Consider the stranger who offers exactly the words you need to hear or the unexpected pivot that leads you to breathtaking beauty.

The quiet in-between is where your own resilience surprises you by revealing depths of courage you never knew you possessed.

Trust the unplanned, the sacred pivots, and welcome the unexpected visitors into your heart. Let yourself to be surprised by the ordinary magic that surrounds you.

Learning to be surprised is learning to be truly alive, open, receptive, and eternally amazed by the sacred choreography of your own existence.

13. Time - Friend or Foe

Have you ever considered Time a friend? Do you honor it or forget about it? Do you run short of it or disregard it all together?

When Time slips through your fingers, it feels like something you are always chasing. It's like something you never have enough of. When you run short of it, piling too much on your plate, overstuffing your hours; life may begin to feel like a race you can't win.

Your relationship with Time reveals so much about how you move through the world. If you chase it frantically, always five minutes behind, breathless and stressed, time is exhausting. If you ignore it, you may be letting opportunities slip away in a haze of procrastination or resistance.

When you walk with Time as a friend, you recognize its value and its limits.

Savor the moments instead of rushing past them and trust that there is always enough time for what matters most. The magic happens in the space between scheduled events.

Your unplanned moments become the memories you will treasure most but they require a willingness by you to let time breathe. Leave space in your day for life to surprise you.

When you shift your thinking in this direction, Time becomes less about scarcity and more about your presence in each moment. It is less about keeping up and more about truly living.

If you allow Time to control you, you miss the spontaneous moments that allow you to receive life's unexpected gifts.

14. Be Vulnerable, Ask

You don't have to carry every burden alone. The myth of complete self-sufficiency has led many of us to shoulder impossible weight in silence.

True strength lies in your willingness to reach out, to ask, to allow yourself to receive.

There is a quiet courage you carry when you let yourself be seen in the tender, unguarded way that shows the soft underbelly of your truth.

Asking for help is not a weakness. It is an act of power, of self-respect, of trust. When you invite others to walk beside you, you honor their wisdom and open your heart to the shared strength that exists in community.

Trust in the goodness of others and in the strength of your connection to All That Is. When you ask, you create a bridge between your own need and another's gifts.

In asking, you offer another the chance to step into their purpose, to share their wisdom, and to be a part of your sacred journey.

What might shift if you let yourself be supported? There is guidance and wisdom all around you and not just in human form. Reach out to the trees, the wind, the water, and the earth.

Ask the beings of light that surround you and love you to step in and support your journey when the going gets tough.

Being vulnerable and asking for help and guidance doesn't diminish you, it restores you.

Be vulnerable, ask, and watch how your world opens in ways that holding it all together on your own never could.

15. Forgiveness is Freedom

Forgiveness isn't always tidy. It doesn't mean you condone what happened, forget who or what hurt you, or invite someone back into your life that has caused you pain.

Forgiveness is a release, a choice you consciously make to stop dragging all that pain behind you like a shadow that blocks your light.

Every moment you hold on to the energetics of things like resentment, anger, guilt or shame, your energy is tethered to a past that you cannot change. Forgiveness releases the hooks that you are bound to, freeing your spirit from the weight of carrying your own or someone else's actions in your heart.

Sometimes the person you need to forgive is yourself. You can't rewrite the past, but you can stop letting it dictate your present, and you can most certainly write the story ahead of you.

Forgiveness is the gift you give to your own soul. It isn't just for those who may have caused you pain. It is for you, for the life you are still living and the dreams you are still manifesting in your world.

You're not weak for forgiving. You're free to reclaim your strength, declaring that your soul's freedom matters more than your need to be "right" or to hold onto old pain.

In forgiving, you are not surrendering your power, you are stepping fully back into it.

16. The Possibility Inside Uncertainty

Some of the most transformative pivots in your life happen in moments of uncertainty. These are times when you didn't have all the answers, when the next step wasn't clear, or when the future felt more like a blank page than a polished outline.

Think of your uncertainty as a birthplace of possibility. It is in these places of not-knowing that you may discover parts of yourself you never knew existed,

When your usual roadmaps fail you and your comfortable routines dissolve, you are forced to tap into the reserves of your creativity, resilience, and intuition. Call back these resources that may have lain dormant for years and now feel unfamiliar yet hopeful.

Uncertainty strips away your illusions of control and invites you to pay attention to new ways of thinking, creating, even being.

When you can't rely on your autopilot settings, you become more present and attuned to the subtle signals and opportunities you might otherwise miss. Consider that a blank canvas holds every color and a story not yet written, holds infinite endings.

Your soul knows the sacred power of the great mystery. The unknown is not a void to fear, but a field of potential waiting for you to show up.

Let uncertainty be one of your teachers. Consider that the manifestation of your beautiful dream may be waiting just outside your comfort zone. You just need to be still enough and uncertain enough, to finally see it, in the quiet in-between.

17. Embodied Listening

Our bodies hold ancient wisdom that no algorithm can replicate.

Every tight shoulder carries a story. Every flutter in your chest whispers a truth. Even the knots in your stomach serve as an early warning system more sophisticated than any technology man has created.

Embodied listening is the practice of tuning in before the body has to shout from a place of discontent, from being ignored or dismissed as random sensations brushed aside in your rush to keep moving forward.

When your bodies whispers go unheard, they grow louder. Your tension becomes pain, fatigue turns into exhaustion, and dis-ease settles where ease once lived.

When you catch hold of one of those whispers, instead of ignoring it, tune in long enough to pause and ask, *"What are you telling me?"*

Your gut doesn't argue or rationalize; it simply knows. Your heart doesn't overthink; it recognizes what resonates and what feels hollow. Listen in the quiet in-between.

This isn't mystical thinking; it is practical intelligence. Your body processes information faster than conscious thought, integrating countless variables into those moments of knowing that arrive as sudden clarity or persistent unease.

Learning to listen within means that you are honoring these signals, trusting that the wisdom carried in your cells and sinew often sees what your mind is too busy to notice.

The invitation here is simple: pause, breathe, and ask your body what it knows. Then listen, not with your ears, but with your entire being.

18. What You Hold, Holds You

The longer you can hold a positive thought, the stronger the positive energy around you becomes. It's not about forced optimism or denying life's challenges, it's about the gradual shift that happens when you learn to dwell in gratitude, hope, or joy for extended moments rather than fleeting seconds.

Think of your positive thoughts like muscles that strengthen with practice. At first, gratitude might last but a single breath before worry creeps back in. As you consciously return to that feeling of thankfulness, extending it from seconds to minutes, something remarkable begins to happen.

When you practice holding a positive intent, your mind begins to default toward possibility rather than hanging on to your problems.

This isn't about pretending challenges don't exist. It is about you intentionally deciding which thoughts you will water and which you will let wither away. You hold the hose!

Negativity is like the weeds you pull; it grows easily if your garden is left unattended. When you consciously choose to maintain a positive outlook, it becomes your default ground.

This sustained positivity creates a kind of magnetic field around you and your life. Opportunities seem to appear more readily, conversations flow with greater ease. Creative solutions show up where once you could only see obstacles.

A single spark of gratitude, hope, or love, when held and nurtured, will expand into a steady glow that lights your path ahead.

19. Faith in the Unfolding

Optimism is not naïve, it's rooted in strength. It doesn't ignore the reality of your struggles; it holds space for possibility in the midst of tough situations.

When you choose optimism intentionally, you look for the light, you lean toward hope, and you believe in outcomes that you haven't yet dreamed.

Holding onto your faith and optimism is not about denying the darkness that exists around us all. It is about refusing to let it have the final say.

Faith is the inner flashlight that guides you forward, helps you navigate the mysteries with the unknown with steadiness, and illuminates paths your doubt would leave in shadows.

Faith in the unfolding means believing that your story is still being written and the current chapter, however challenging, is not the conclusion nor anywhere close to the end. It's a deep knowing that even when you can't see the path ahead, you are held by something greater than your immediate circumstances.

When you choose this powerful perspective, you become an active participant in your own transformation rather than a passive victim of your circumstance. Faith in an optimistic unfolding transforms you from someone to whom things happen into someone who dances with life's mysterious rhythms, trusting that even the most difficult steps are leading somewhere worth going.

Let your imagination answer with vision and faith. Optimism is not passive, it's a quiet act of bravery in a world that often wants proof before belief. Believe…

20. Walking with Wonder

Wonder is not reserved for a newborn's smile or a rainbow that appears after a long winter storm. It lives in the quiet space between one breath and the next, in the way that sunlight catches dust particles dancing through your window, or in the intricate architecture of a spider's web dripping with sparkles after a spring rain.

The magic you seek is not hiding in distant places or in hidden spaces. It is woven into each moment of your day, just waiting for eyes willing to see.

To walk with wonder is to move through the world open-eyed and open-hearted, willing to be surprised. It's choosing to notice the shimmer of the ordinary and to let the extraordinary brush up against you like a friendly wind.

Walking with wonder means moving through your days as an explorer in familiar territory, recognizing that presence transforms the ordinary into the extraordinary.

When you slow down enough to step into this expanded way of seeing, you will catch glimpses of the miracles that are always occurring.

You will remember that you are walking through magic disguised as an ordinary day, and realize it was never hiding. You were just moving too fast to see it.

Every step you take in wonder strengthens your connection to the very magic of life's unfolding artistry. The more you notice, the more there is to see.

21. Embracing Life's Detours

Life rarely unfolds as planned. The straight road you imagined often bends into unexpected curves, sacred pivots as I call them, some sharp, some gentle. These pivots can feel like delays or disappointments. More often, they are the quiet teachers that lead you to unexpected treasures.

What you encounter as a detour may just be directing you onto the main road that has been disguised. These redirected moments often carry gifts that your original plans would never have delivered.

Consider the possibility that these sacred pivots are leading you to wisdom that only comes through traveling down paths you didn't choose.

In this unfamiliar territory, where your carefully drawn map no longer applies, you discover skills you didn't realize you had.

You find courage you didn't know you could summon as you see from a different point of view, a perspective that broadens your world.

Breathe deeply into the mystery. What might this turn be offering?

When you learn to trust the path ahead, even when it twists and turns, you discover that life's magic often hides in the places you never meant to go, beyond the fog that hides the path.

The destination is not lost. You are simply being guided toward it in a way your soul can truly follow.

22. Drifting or Directing

When you set an intention for whatever you are doing, you are corralling those thoughts that tend to scatter every which direction. You will capture your ideas as they come and go, start and stop, get a handle on the ones that jump about from one second to the next with no rhythm or reason.

Left unattended, your mind is like a field of dandelions, easily carried away on the next breeze that blows through.

Your intention acts like an anchor, rooting your energy in the direction you choose. It doesn't involve some grand plan, it can be set with a single word, a quiet phrase, or a clear image in your mind that guides your attention and shapes the path ahead. Setting an intention, daily or even minute by minute, brings you present in that moment.

Consciously focusing on your purpose reminds you why you are doing what you are doing and helps you return to your center when distractions pull you away.

Pay attention as you set your intentions. Without them, you will still move forward in your journey, but you may arrive in places that hold no meaning for you and the path you are traveling.

You might ask yourself, each morning, *"Where do I want my energy to flow today?"* Follow your answer and with it, even the smallest action can carry purpose as your day becomes a reflection of what matters most to you.

Set your intentions daily, nurture them continually, hold them gently, and like a compass in your hand, let them point you toward the life you want to live.

23. The Truth You've Outgrown

Old truths don't always stay true. Beliefs that once protected you can become cages. Roles you played out of necessity can become costumes that no longer fit.

There is courage in acknowledging when you have grown beyond the containers that once held you. The stories you told yourself about who you were, what you deserved, what was possible… were narratives that served a holy purpose at the time you "wrote" them into your story. They were the cocoon that protected your becoming and the scaffolding that supported your early construction of self.

Your soul's journey is one of perpetual expansion. What felt like an absolute truth at twenty, might feel too small at thirty, forty, or beyond. The voice that whispered "you are not enough" may have motivated you to push on. Now it stands in the way of an updated version of yourself.

Letting go of your old beliefs is part of your human evolution. It is the natural rhythm of a life lived fully, where each phase of understanding prepares you for the next. Some say, "The butterfly does not dishonor the caterpillar by taking flight; it fulfills the caterpillar's deepest purpose."

Release yourself from the obligation to remain consistent with who you used to be. Some beliefs, like some folks in our lives, are here for a reason, a season, or a lifetime.

You are not required to fit into yesterday's version of yourself.

You are invited to shed those old stories and step into the truth of who you are meant to be now. Let these truths you've outgrown fall away with grace, and trust that something wiser is rising in their place.

24. Seek Serenity in Stillness

There is a sanctuary waiting for you that requires no reservation, costs you nothing, and is always available. It is the profound peace that is found in genuine stillness.

This is not the stillness of exhaustion or boredom, it is an intentional quiet where wisdom waits to be heard and your deepest knowing can finally speak above the internal chatter that so often drowns it out.

In stillness, you will discover that serenity or peace, isn't something you "can get to," it is something you remember. Stillness lies in the recognition that beneath all your thoughts, worries, and endless mind chatter there lies a vast quiet place that is spacious, aware, and inherently peaceful.

It isn't a place that you need to create, it just needs to be "uncovered," like clearing a rockslide from a path you know lies beneath the piles of rubble.

When you allow yourself to sink into true stillness, something profound shifts. You relax, your breath slows, your shoulders drop, and you loosen your grip on everyday concerns as your own inner clarity emerges.

Answers to questions you've been searching for suddenly seem obvious. Creativity bubbles up out of nowhere and sparks your imagination as if it had been waiting patiently for the noise to settle so it could finally be heard.

This is where wisdom lives, in the fertile silence where your own truth is heard. In stillness you remember that you already know more than you think you know.

The guidance you seek isn't outside of you, it is already present within the quiet chambers of your own being, in the silence of your sacred sanctuary.

25. The Journey is Uniquely Yours

It's natural to glance over at the neighbor or look over someone else's shoulder, comparing their journey to yours. You "see" their success, or joy, or it feels like they got it all right and somehow you have fallen behind.

Your journey was never meant to mirror anyone else's, It is uniquely yours, exquisitely tailored to your own be-coming.

Your journey will rarely be linear. It is an ever-upward spiraling ascension of your human spirit leading you toward wisdom, wholeness, and joy.

The Divine has crafted your path with sacred precision, blending the exact experiences, challenges and revelations that your soul needs for its evolution. What feels like a struggle today may be creating the very friction you need to move forward on your intended path.

What feels like a delay is just divine timing preparing you for gifts you haven't been ready to receive. Spirit may be waiting to impart wisdom to you that you are now growing strong enough to carry.

Lean into trust and let go of the old story that says you are supposed to be somewhere else by now.

Your unique journey is just that, uniquely yours. Trust that your path is sacred even when it looks nothing like anyone else's. Envision the hand of Spirit on your back gently guiding you down the perfect path to your becoming exactly who you were always meant to become.

26. The Spacious Heart of Humility

Humility invites you to keep learning, keep listening, and keep growing. It doesn't diminish your light, rather it helps you hold it with reverence. You don't have to shrink to be sincere or disappear to be humble.

True humility is spacious. It makes room for others, for change, and for wisdom to move smoothly in and out of your world.

You can be deeply rooted in your sacred gifts and still be teachable. You can walk soundly with your purpose and still say, "I don't know everything." In fact, that very openness to "more" is what makes you trustworthy, relatable, authentic, and real.

This spacious humility creates a magnetic quality that draws people toward truth rather than performance. When you can hold your expertise lightly, without the armor of needing to be right, you become a safe harbor for others vulnerability.

In this way, humility becomes a gift not just to yourself, but to everyone who encounters your presence.

When you are not defending your image or protecting your ego, your energy becomes available for deeper listening, genuine connections, and clearer sight. Perhaps most beautifully, humility allows you to hold space for the mystery of not-knowing while still offering what you do know with confidence.

It's the sweet spot where certainty dances with curiosity and your light shines brightest precisely because you are not trying so hard to prove it exists.

When your heart stays open and your ego stays light, you become a living invitation for truth to be spoken, for wisdom to be shared, and for grace to quietly change the room.

27. You Are Always Becoming

Life is a journey down roads planned and unexpected trails. There is no final arrival, no point where growth stops and perfection begins. You are not a finished work of art but a living masterpiece, simultaneously the creator and the creation of yourself.

Each experience, every joy, every heartache, writes a chapter in your ongoing story. Even at times when you felt lost, something deep within you was quietly transforming.

This endless road to becoming is not a design flaw but the very heart of what makes you unique and magnificently human. You are both the sculptor and the clay, the artist and the canvas, the writer and the page.

Every day you wake up just a little bit different than you were the day before. Sometimes it will be in ways so subtle they escape your notice and other times; the difference will come in shifts so profound they will redefine everything you thought you knew about yourself.

Those moments that feel like endings might just be beginnings in disguise. Every version of yourself that you outgrow doesn't disappear. They become the foundation of who you will be next.

There is true freedom in embracing this eternal becoming. You can release yourself from the perpetual pursuit of your perfect self and fall in love with the beautiful, messy, ever-unfolding process of your own evolution.

Today's version of you is both complete and incomplete, whole in this moment and at the same time preparing to bloom into someone even more authentic tomorrow. Enjoy the journey.

28. Embracing Change

The one constant you can count on in this life is change. Our elders and their ancestors knew it. They answered the question posed by their youngsters when asked, "Why is this or that happening?" by reminding them that, "The world is changing."

Resistance often shows up when change is underway. You find yourself backing away from new experiences or releasing old ones because you are uncomfortable or uncertain about things.

Remember when you feel resistance rise, true change is the foundation upon which your evolutionary development will grow.

Change is inevitable, for without it, you would remain stuck in patterns that would keep you planted right where you are, doing just what you've been doing, with no forward momentum on your journey.

Consider changing your point of view and when overwhelm or anxiety comes calling, turn around and face them with curiosity. Consider them an invitation for you to grow and bloom.

Even the most unexpected changes carry with them hidden opportunities, golden moments that are there for your taking.

Lean into change with an open heart and welcome it with optimism and joy. Embrace it and celebrate change as a catalyst for your personal growth and evolution.

29. Wisdom Walks with You

You do not walk this path alone. Though unseen, wisdom moves beside you like an old friend, steady and patient. Sometimes it arrives as a sudden knowing or a clear inner voice. Other times it whispers through the eyes of someone who believes in you, or through the whispers in the wind.

Wisdom is not only found in grand revelations; it is in the small choices that honor your heart, in the moments that keep you grounded, in the courage it takes to walk on even when the path ahead is unclear.

Wisdom is visible in the way you return to yourself after being pulled off course. It is in the very breath you take before speaking.

Wisdom is in the grace you extend to someone, even yourself, when it would be easier to turn away. These are not small things, they are the very things that keep your soul aligned with its true course.

Let yourself feel it, this presence that guides, nudges, and sometimes carries you. Wisdom has been with you since before you could name it. It is woven into your soul, an inheritance of light and learning that grows each time you listen.

Trust that every step you take, no matter how uncertain, is a step taken hand in hand with something sacred. Wisdom walks with you, always.

30. A Place Between Moments

There is a place we don't talk about often. It isn't marked on any calendar or to-do list.

You won't find it in the noise of your busy-ness or in the clamor of others expectations.

It is there… in that quiet in-between, just before your next breath or right after a tear falls.

It might show up in the light that dances on your wall or when something inside tells you that you have crossed a threshold or moved through a gateway you didn't even know was waiting for you.

These are the sacred in-between moments. It is a quiet place, unassuming and yet infinitely rich.

It is where you remember you, not the version molded by others demands or expectations, but the truest you, the one who breathes without effort.

In this still space, you can hear the whispers of wisdom that often get lost in the rush of your everyday life.

It is here that you may feel the weight of your worries lift away and sense that life holds you more tenderly than you had realized. Let yourself linger here in this quiet in- between moment. Let your mind soften and your spirit stretch wide.

You do not have to do anything to enter this place. Simply notice it. Let it remind you that life is not only found in the doing, but also in the gentle pause of being in the sacred now. Here, you are enough, you are whole.

It is here you find the Quiet In-Between.

The Mystery Is the Way, Unmapped and Unafraid

Some of life's most profound breakthroughs come in the moments when you stop needing every answer. The mystery itself becomes a path, a practice, a presence. It leads not through clarity, but through wonder, unmapped.

When the plan disappears and the map doesn't match the terrain, there is still a compass; your truth, your intuition, your breath. Take the next step, unafraid.

Being unmapped is not being lost. It is simply being willing to walk without guarantees. It is honoring that not everything sacred can be planned. It is allowing the road to rise beneath your feet, even if you don't yet know where it's taking you.

The mystery doesn't ask you to figure it out. It asks you to show up with open eyes, with bare feet, and with the courage to say: I don't know what this is, but I will walk it anyway.

The Heart of it All

You have just walked, word by word, through thirty sacred moments, small doorways of presence, truth, and unfolding. None of them were asking you to be better, to do more, or to finally "get it right." They were offering something far more precious: an opportunity to show up for your own becoming.

This is the heart of it, isn't it? A life lived with the quiet in-between, in the space between moments. A life where quiet courage meets honest reflection, where you meet yourself not in perfection, but in presence.

Carry these moments with you gently. Let them work their way into your breath, your rhythms, your choices. Let them become companions, not commands. You are already whole, already wise. You are already walking in the direction of your own sacred unfolding.

A Closing Prayer

May you meet each moment with a quiet heart.

May you honor the pauses as much as the progress.

May you remember that grace lives in the quiet in-between.

May your breath be a doorway to presence.

May your courage be enough, even when it's quiet.

May your journey be blessed.

About the Author

As the founder of Wisdom Evolution and head cheerleader for The You First Revolution, Vicki Dobbs has been helping people navigate their lives and business in a way that allows them to gift the world with the best of themselves. She specializes in writing and crafting virtual and in-person courses that include some form of sacred creativity or art to anchor the teaching given, into the participants' physical world.

Introducing ancient wisdom techniques blended with modern modalities through experiential classes, ceremony, sacred art, and story, Vicki's goal is to see everyone live every day empowered by the voice of their own authentic truth.

Using her international best-selling books, courses, and work with individuals or speaking to groups, she endeavors to inspire others to create their lives intentionally.

At its heart, Vicki's business is about inspiring self-discovery, personal evolution, and spiritual empowerment. Teaching the sacred art of choosing "you first," her programs are designed to help you discover who you are beyond what you do. Using shamanic journey work, guided visualizations, sacred art, creative writing and journal work, you have an opportunity to "meet" who you are and design the path to who you are becoming, and who you will be.

Website: https://vickidobbs.com

Facebook: https://www.facebook.com/vickildobbsauthor/

Instagram: https://www.instagram.com/vickidobbs/

Pinterest: https://pinterest.com/vickidobbs33/

https://www.linkedin.com/in/vicki-l-dobbs/

Email: vicki@vickidobbs.com

Other Books by Vicki L. Dobbs

Get Off the Shelf: You Have a Right to be Happy

You First: Practical Wisdom for Nurturing Body, Mind, Heart, and Soul

Wisdom and Wit: A Little Life Book

The Power of Gratitude Journal

Introducing the Gifts of Our Good Enemies: Reframing the Challenges and Frustrations We All Encounter

Please use these following pages to capture your reflections, ah-ha moments, or the thoughts that spring up as you read.

www.ingramcontent.com/pod-product-compliance
Lightning Source LLC
Chambersburg PA
CBHW071020080526
44587CB00015B/2436